THE
Smarts

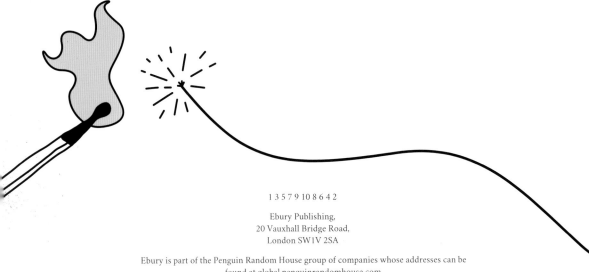

1 3 5 7 9 10 8 6 4 2

Ebury Publishing,
20 Vauxhall Bridge Road,
London SW1V 2SA

Ebury is part of the Penguin Random House group of companies whose addresses can be
found at global.penguinrandomhouse.com

First published in the United Kingdom by Ebury Publishing in 2019

www.penguin.co.uk

A CIP catalogue record for this book is available from the British Library

ISBN 9781785042454

Design and illustration by Karen Lilje, Hybrid Creative

Printed and bound in China by Toppan Leefung

Penguin Random House is committed to a sustainable future for our business, our readers
and our planet. This book is made from Forest Stewardship Council® certified paper.

THE
Smarts

BIG LITTLE HACKS TO TAKE YOU
A LONG WAY AT WORK

SAJ JETHA

To my master Smarties: Mum, Dad and Khairunnisa.

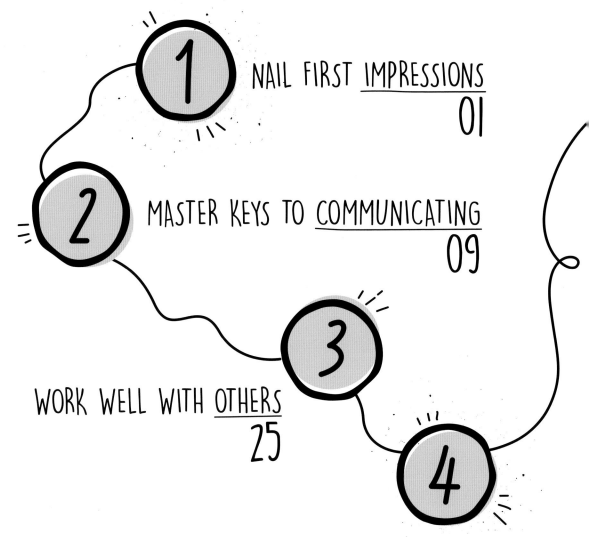

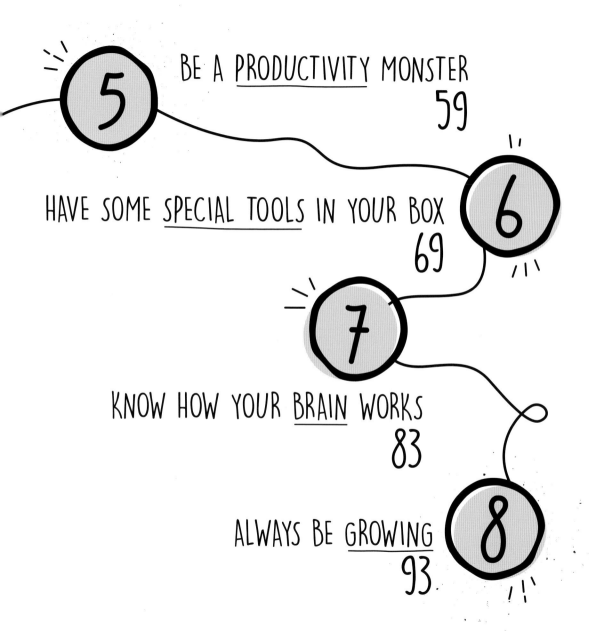

THE SMARTS

SOMEONE WHO POSSESSES THE SMARTS

SMARTY

THINKING, FEELING AND DOING
TO GET RESULTS AT WORK

SMARTIES

PEOPLE WHO POSSESS THE SMARTS

THE SMARTS: WHAT ARE THEY?

Whether you're starting your first job, moving to a new one or just trying to break out of the same-old, there are ways of working that can give you a big advantage. I call these the smarts, and the people who use them are Smarties.

Smarties have cracked – *hacked* – work with the smarts. They cut through the noise, understanding the small things that really help achieve mastery. Smarties do things right, and they do the right things. Their mastery brings results – which, at the risk of cliché, can change the world.

Years ago, figuring out the smarts was a matter of necessity for me. I was born into an immigrant family and was the first to get a job in 'The City'. I needed to understand mastery at work, fast!

This led me on an adventure to discover precisely what the smarts are. Over the years I've found them everywhere from the boardrooms of leading companies to crisis response units. From the trading floor to the operating table.

I've grown to understand how Smarties communicate, work with others and with themselves. I've also seen how they come up smiling irrespective of what the crazy world of work chooses to throw at them.

I became *so* excited about the power of smarts that I set up a company called The Smarty Train. Together with an inspirational team, we have trained tens of thousands of Smarties, helping them to unlock their talent every day. We've worked with some of the biggest brands in the world and even picked up a few awards along the way.

But now it's time for you to learn the smarts and put their power to use. Enjoy your adventure: if it's anything like mine, it's going to be brilliant.

Saj Jetha

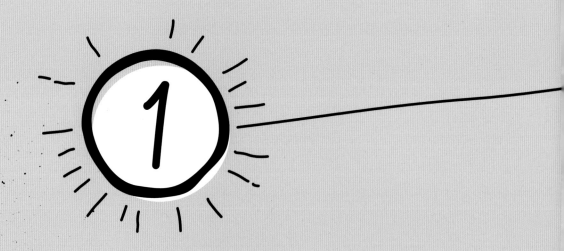

NAIL

FIRST IMPRESSIONS

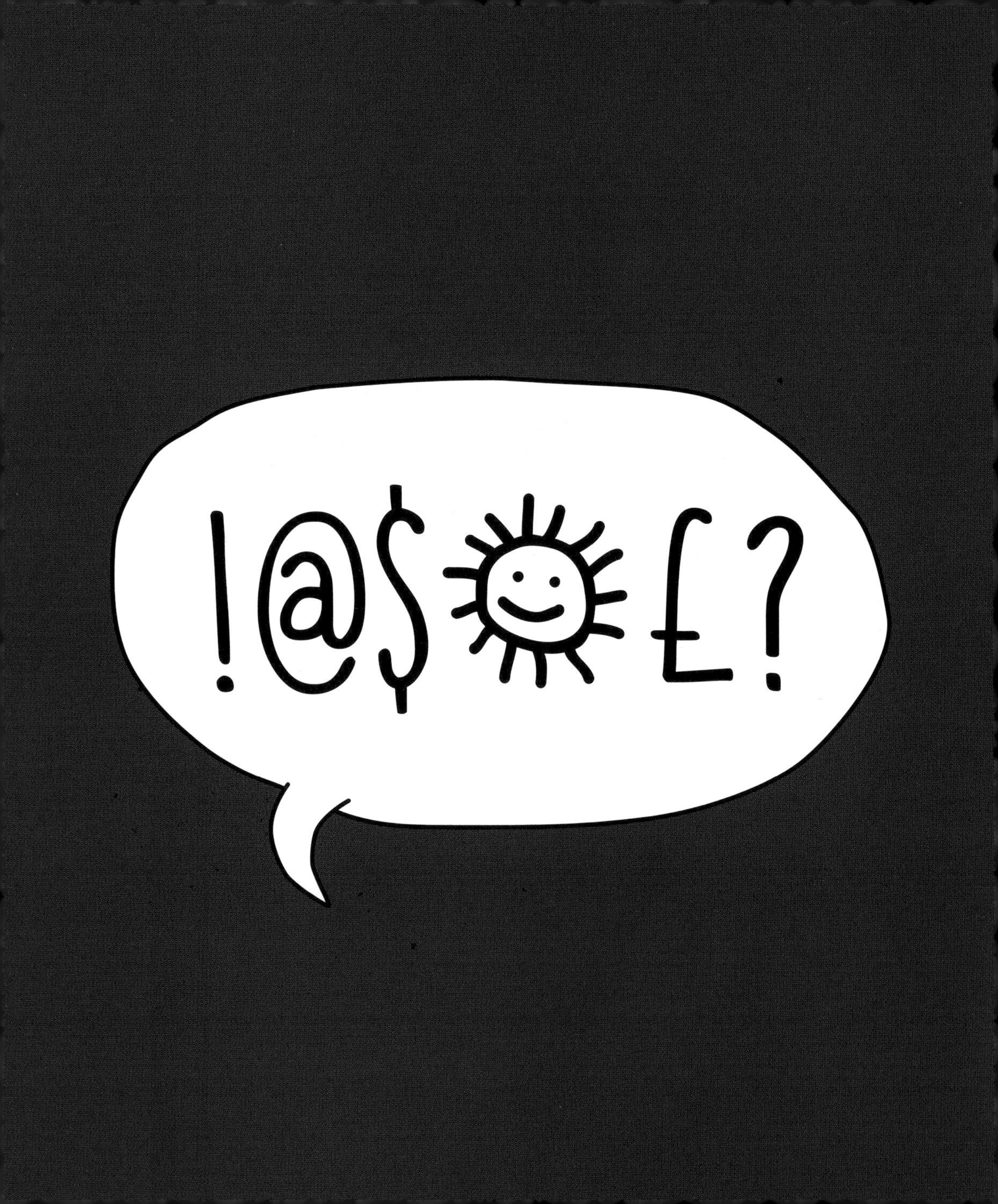

WTF

Stuck for something to say? Cat got your tongue? Want to make a connection? Think: WTF.

No really. Work, Travel, Fun. Three sure-fire conversation starters that will keep you chatting for an hour or more with someone.

Don't worry if it feels trite and unimportant to begin with. Smarties know that small talk may lead on to big talk.

WTF: Just try it.

OMG. It'll work.

THAT FIRST ENCOUNTER ——————

First encounters are always scary no matter what the pros say. You're desperate to present the best side of you, but fearful you're projecting the worst. It doesn't help that your internal system behaves a bit differently to normal, just when you need it to be at its sharpest. The intense focus on you means you won't have the ability to do the thing that matters most in a first encounter. The thing that makes you a Smarty.

When the introductions are made, you may not remember names.

Here are some tips for that first encounter:

1. Really listen when a person says their name (remember, your nerves are at an all-time high in this exact moment).
2. When you hear it, repeat it back and try and make an association with it that is personal to you: 'My friend's also called Sarah', or 'How are you spelling Laila, with an i or a y?'
3. Repeat the person's name back before the end of your encounter.
4. (Bonus marks: Repeat it to yourself an hour later to get it into your long-term memory).
5. If your first encounter happens to be around a table with lots of other people, draw yourself a table plan with the names of your new encounters.

HELLO. MY NAME IS...

_ _ _ _ _ _ _ _ _

Remembering someone's name is the Smarty way to connect and build a rapport. It's a little thing, but a big one.

T MINUS

The countdown period to a rocket launch is crucial. Key events take place at each milestone, data is analysed, questions that need answers are answered.

Without this vital period, there can be no spectacular launch.

Give yourself some launch time; work a countdown period into each key event. Conference call? Dial in five minutes early to ensure everything is working. Meeting? Be the first to get there. You'll get the chance to speak informally to others before diving into work. Don't forget travel time when planning.

Smarties always start work a little early every day.* It gives them time to think, focus on the tasks ahead and plan how to tackle them.

Build T minus into your everyday routine. Be early in proportion to what is about to happen. Think how long you will need to get tuned in and give yourself the right platform to perform at your best.

···5···4···3···2··| *For a rocketing head start, perfect your countdown.*

* Or they look at their diaries before closing down, seeing what's coming tomorrow and planning for it.

KNOW THE VITALS

Smarties can sum up what's happening where they work in half a dozen words. They know its vital signs inside out.

Traditional medics are trained to relay a patient's vitals at any given moment. You need to be able to do the same. The terms (and numbers) that drive your business should be imprinted on your brain and always ready to go.

Learn them. Understand them. Watch how they change, progress or retreat. Be prepared to reel them off whenever necessary without hesitation should someone ask you something.

Work vitals are not the difference between life and death, but they are crucial to your work and your relationship with it.

At the bare minimum, the vitals you should know about are: your organisation's current values, vision and strategy, the problems it tries to solve, its leaders, its revenues (and targets and financial drivers, if applicable), stock performance (if applicable), what your organisation asks of its people and any big projects it has on.

Cherish the vitals – they'll keep your career healthy, too.

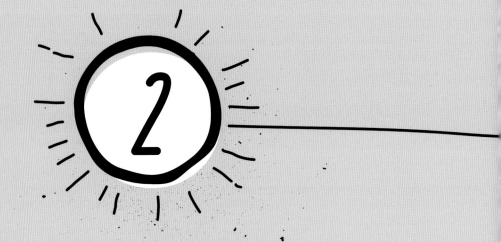

MASTER

KEYS TO COMMUNICATING

WHAT NOT WHO

Imagine the best advice you've ever been given from someone you like. Now think of someone you really dislike, and picture that same advice coming from them. Which one is easier on the ears?

And herein lies the problem: people generally trump perspective.

To be a Smarty, separate the perspective from the person. Listen to what is being said, not who is saying it.

Put another way: the next time you're in a situation and the music is not to your tune, focus on the song, not the singer. When you give it a fresh hearing you might find it on your wavelength after all.

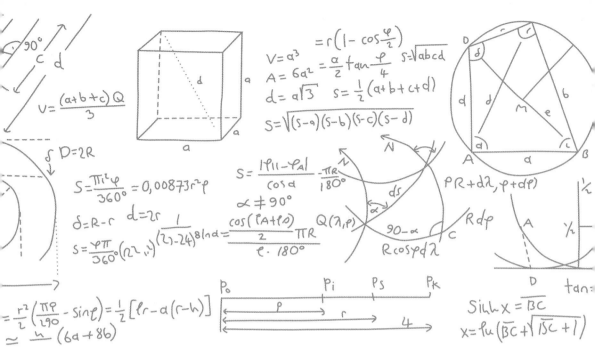

CHECKING AND VALIDATING

Smarty conversations happen when you check and validate. Your manager asks you for an update. Two minutes into your response stop and ask: 'Am I going into the right level of detail?'

The questioner might only have wanted a couple of words: it's going well, or I've encountered a few issues but I'm dealing with them. Or, they may have wanted to dive even deeper into the detail. By checking and validating in the early stages of the answer you will give them exactly what they wanted from the interaction. And who wouldn't want that?

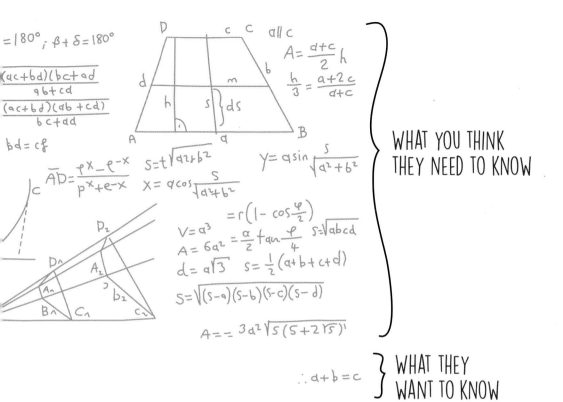

WHAT YOU THINK
THEY NEED TO KNOW

WHAT THEY
WANT TO KNOW

Dial up, or dial down, or make no change; ask if they want the scenic route or the highway. You'll both get to where you want to be faster.

Checking and validating could be used in lots of your interactions at work. Many things going wrong (or not being right) are because of an absence of it.

BREVITY IS BEST*

This sentence has exactly six words. It's a good sentence length, right? It gets the point across perfectly. I'm sure that everyone will agree. So why do so many people insist on writing really, really long sentences, with hugely descriptive language, to get across a point about their work when it often just distracts from the entire point under discussion? Writing in shorter sentences wins respect.

Speak with brevity. Make your points quickly and sharply. Be that person everyone wants to hear from because you've thought clearly about what you want to say.

Take out words you really don't need. Waste words and you will be wasting your colleague's time.

 If it takes too long to get to the point, you never will make it. You don't want that.

TELLING STORIES —————————

To make what you say sticky, perfect the craft of telling a truly memorable story. Use hooks or analogies, pose a question, or come at it from an unexpected angle. Think about the weight of every word. Focus on helping the listener to visualise what you mean.

We're assailed on a daily basis with words, opinions, information and DETAIL. But not all of it (in fact, often very little) means anything unless you join it up.

You don't need to talk a lot, or use big words, to be a Smarty. Just paint a colourful, vivid picture by telling good stories.

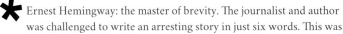 Ernest Hemingway: the master of brevity. The journalist and author was challenged to write an arresting story in just six words. This was it. It tells you everything you need to know. Sadly.

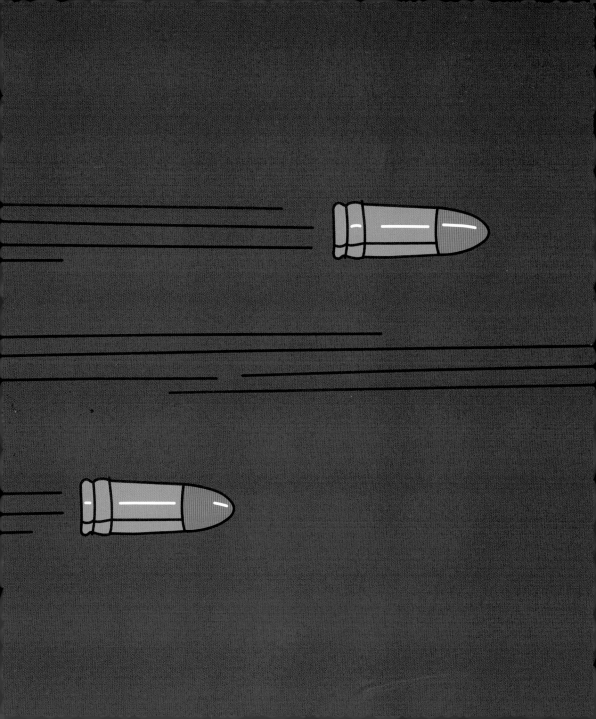

WHY NOT WHY?

It's only three letters, but it packs a powerful punch. In fact, the word 'Why' is like a bullet to the brain and can stop a thought process or dialogue in its track if used unthinkingly.

Why creates an atmosphere that is sometimes hostile and combative. It can sound like a challenge, which practically invites an objection or stall.

Smarties appreciate the importance of the question 'why' but use it carefully.

They consider when to use it and when to mask its use. How? If using it directly they ensure someone is warmed up enough before going in for the swoop. They also think about the tone with which they say it. And if not using it directly, they ask it in a different way with an open tone:

'Can you explain your reasoning, to help me understand?'

This more indirect approach invites a different type of dialogue while also getting you to your why.

Why not think about how you're using 'why'?

seɪ wɒt juː miːn

(SAY WHAT YOU MEAN)

Are you **ANGRY** or just a little irritated? Is this project **REALLY, REALLY, STRESSING YOU OUT**, or are you just a little nervous you're not taking the right approach. It's great you are **SUPER EXCITED** about this, but you seem to be pretty excited about most things. Maybe you are just comfortable with the direction we're taking?

Spoken language is a powerful force. It can be cyclical too, because the words we use dictate our reactions to the events we describe.

If a person complains of feeling stressed, they may feel as though they are living on a knife-edge. They may even feel resentful of the supposed source of that stress. It will affect their interactions in every sphere. However, if this 'stressed' person stopped to think for a moment, they may realise the emotion they are feeling isn't really stress at all. It may be nerves over the direction things are taking, or even worry that they may not be the right person for the job. Coming at things with the right words changes everything.

Words really do matter.

It's very easy to retreat into the comfort of a handful of well-worn adjectives. We are all guilty of using them as a shorthand to describe our emotions. If you do, you are doing yourself a disservice.

Google the *Harvard Business Review* article by author, speaker and advisor Susan David on '3 Ways to Better Understand your Emotions'. It includes a handy table to help you better identify exactly what you are feeling and better judge the intensity of emotions and the words to describe them.

Now that is something to be EXCITED about, but also THANKFUL, RELIEVED and definitely more CONFIDENT.

START
HERE

PROGRESS, PLANS AND PROBLEMS[1]

Everyone asks for updates at work. All the time. Smarties know there are only three elements required to report on, so be prepared to do so on a whim.

Smarty Status Report: Progress, plans, problems.

Nothing else required.

Need an example? 'How's the report you're working on going?'

Progress: *'Last week, I achieved...*

Plans: *'This week I plan to...'*

Problems: *'Where I have an issue is...'*

(Thanks to 6-year-old Amelia for helping us test that the maze is solvable.)

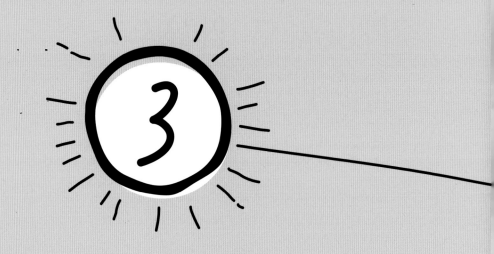

WORK

WELL WITH OTHERS

TEST

Do this simple test. Ask someone to watch you as you draw a capital E on your forehead. Now turn this book upside down to see why I asked you to do it.

Did you draw your E in a way that anyone looking at it could read it? Or did you trace the letter so it faced you?

The reason for asking you to do this test says a lot about your ability to imagine things from someone else's perspective, otherwise known as empathy.

Those that write the E so it is legible to others are more likely to take the perspective of those around them. Those that focus on writing a letter readable to themselves might be less likely to.

Smarties see things from the point of view of others. They use language that shows it. They know that seeing the world from someone else's perspective changes everything. If you tune into another's perspective you'll be in a stronger position. Not only that, it'll show them that their needs are a priority.

How often are you seeing the world from others' perspective? Which way is your E being drawn?

Be the right E.

COMPLETE THE CONTEXT JIGSAW

Starting a conversation without understanding the context is like beginning a jigsaw without checking you've got all the pieces. Just a single missing piece – of context or jigsaw – changes everything.

In any given situation, Smarties take the time to ask and understand, 'What's going on?'

Replies may reveal that a colleague is suddenly under pressure to complete a task in record time, or is feeling under the weather, or is battling to sort out a major issue. It could be that the organisation has just missed a major target, won a major prize or had a big story hit the news. This is all essential context to what happens next in *your* conversation with them. It could be the reason why your chat didn't land in the way you thought it would. Or your brilliant presentation worked last week but not this week.

Nothing at work operates in a vacuum. Everything is linked. Everything is connected. Try and understand what's going on first, and during, something. It's what will make you a Smarty.

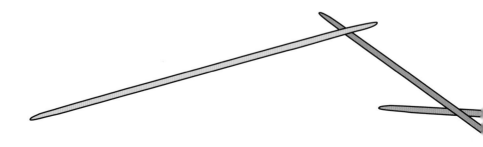

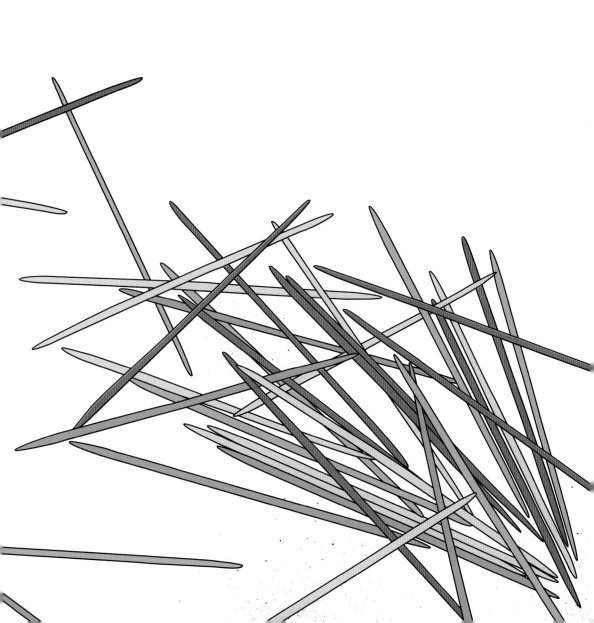

TIMING IS EVERYTHING ————

In an experiment, judges' verdicts almost always went in an applicant's favour after lunch, or a short break. 'Good' decisions dropped off precipitously as the afternoon wore on.[3]

In this case it is hunger that might be causing the 'wrong' decision.* But there are lots of other factors that can cause you not to reach the outcome you want. It might be when you ask for something, how you ask, and what is going on for a person just before you ask.

Smarties observe people's habits.** Choose your moment. There are 'good' and 'bad' times for everyone. Think about those moments when someone's just come off a call and is processing its content. Or maybe when someone's en route to that meeting and preparing in their head. Or even if they're just off to get that well-needed coffee. All not good times if you're looking for a positive interaction.

     * Apparently I get 'hangry' sometimes. Being angry when I get hungry doesn't always get me the outcome that I, or more importantly others, want.

    **Advanced Smarty. Observe your own habits, too.

THINKING ABOUT THINKING?

There is a real distinction between asking someone what they think, versus what they are thinking. Think about it.

Asking a person what they *think* is a knock-out blow. It provokes a definitive all-or-nothing response. You'll know the direction that person is taking. It's usually firm and clear. The downside is you don't hear about the elements that prompted them to take that path.

Inquiring about someone's *thinking* is powerfully different. It demands less commitment to the end result, though you'll probably get one. Intriguing thought processes are unveiled. Those who might be nervous of giving an answer are more willing to verbally weigh up the pros and cons.

Both are open questions, but Smarties know the second approach guarantees so much more (read about open questions on page 75). Thinking about thinking is a valuable learning tool.

Tomorrow, when you come out of a meeting, ask those around you what they are thinking. Their reflections will deepen your understanding, giving you insight into the process as well as the outcome.

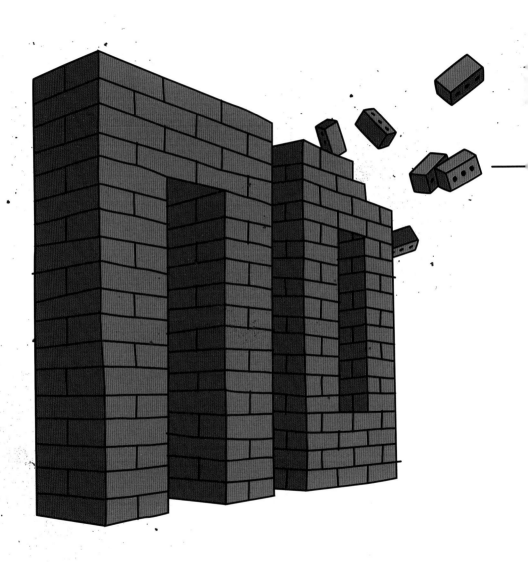

SMASH DOWN BRICK WALLS

'No' is an absolute brick wall of resistance. It's easy to say,
but once it is out there, it is almost impossible to break down.

It pulls a conversation up short, stops it in its tracks and kills all hope of a resolution.
It has no grey area.

Smarties lead the way by understanding how to say 'no' differently. They are the
masters of the alternative no. It keeps the dialogue and future possibilities open, and
the walls transparent. Think of it as the gift that keeps giving.

They say something like: 'Thank you for asking. I really wish I could work with you on
this. It sounds like a great opportunity and one I would learn from. Sadly, I'm committed
to X this month and it's a priority. Definitely keep me in mind next time though.'

The path forward is kept clear. You're not associated with eliciting the reaction that
'no' often causes. The door is left more open.

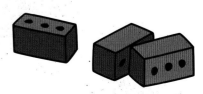

WHICH HAT SHOULD YOU WEAR?

We are asked to play many different roles at work. On any one day, you might be the details person, the structure person, the challenger, the tone person… the list goes on. For maximum effectiveness, get into the right character from the off.

When a Smarty is asked to contribute they ask:

'What role would you like me to play here, in order to help you the most?'

While it's tempting to jump in and go the extra mile, the true value is always in ensuring you are doing what's being asked of you.

You may have been invited to go over a document simply to proof it for spelling and grammar. Alternatively, the person who asked for your input may feel you'd be a great fresh pair of eyes to see it from the recipient's perspective – is anything missing? Will this be understood in different geographies? There are a myriad of reasons you may be brought in. Ask.

If you don't play your part, at best you'll irritate your colleague. At worst they'll know never to ask you again. Ouch.

YOU

YOU

BLAME GAME

Everyone screws up. All the time. Even a Smarty. When a project goes awry it is 100 per cent likely you played a part in what went wrong. Yes, 100 per cent. Even if you only had 0.005 per cent of a role.

Own it!

Don't get distracted by spinning the wheel on the blame game. Sure, it's addictive, but it's super-destructive too. It takes your focus and emotional energy, and things often become irreparable once you start to blame. Even if someone appears to be pointing fingers, rise above it and focus on the real issue. It'll open your mind to having a sensible conversation about putting things right, either this time, or the next.

Smarties reframe blame by owning their contribution and focusing on the issue at hand.

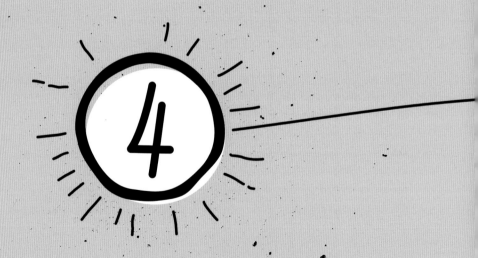

BECOME

AN EXPERT IN HOW YOU WORK

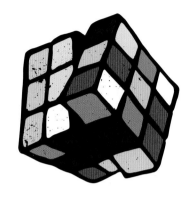

MEETING OF MINDS

Top sports players never start a game from cold. They always warm up before the big game and that gets results. Can you put aside the time to warm up before your big game?

Take meetings as a case in point. All too often meetings have become a euphemism for: I don't have time to think about this, so let's have a meeting. Everyone turns up cold and nothing gets done.

Meetings should count, not just be a body count.
What if you could use meetings to save time and get better results?

The moment the meeting invite lands, start the warm-up and ask yourself:

'How do I form a perspective before I attend the meeting?'
'What do I need to form that perspective?'

These two questions will make you do what you need to do and think about what you need to think. This is the warm-up that Smarties carry out. Watch how your meetings change when you go into one with a perspective.

If people relate to your perspective, you will move forward (and you've saved everyone time). If they don't, you still move forward, but in a different way now!

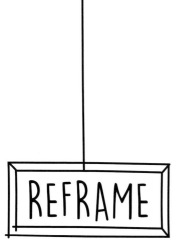

REFRAME

'I' can be the sweetest-sounding word.
After all, who doesn't like to talk about themselves?

Beware though: it can have negative connotations for how you work and see the world sometimes.[4]

'I've been in this job six weeks and I don't think it is going that well. I keep getting more and more complex projects. I didn't really expect all this...'

Reframe the same scenario in the third person and objectively. (It sounds a bit weird to start with, but persevere.)

'Aisha has only been here a while and she's still finding her feet. She's been doing well with the projects being offered to her, so has started to get more complex ones. She's got a lot more on her plate than she expected – but she is open to the challenge...'

This objective version helps you. It gives you room to manoeuvre. It ditches the negativity and gives a Smarty space to grow.

BEWARE OF YOUR HOOK ZONE

You just love putting together videos. Or maybe you're a genius with a spreadsheet, or crafting a slideshow. Colleagues will queue at your desk, clutching their clips, or data. You'll be the go-to person because you've got the hammer when everyone else has a nail. What a buzz. You're in your Hook Zone.

And therein lies the problem.

Hook Zones should come with a big health warning. It's great being good at something. There really is no better feeling. Yet, it's easy to get carried away doing what you like, to the detriment of all else. You'll become a one-trick pony as your attention is easily 'caught' tuning into those Hook moments. There are two implications. The non-hook work is still your job and needs to get done – now just with less time. The second is you're not learning new stuff. Be sure to keep taking yourself out of your comfort zone.

Don't give up being the best at something. Just recognise the signs of being hooked and keep your balance in check.

LET IT GO

When something bad happens, not everything is **THE END OF THE WORLD!!**

A wise friend of mine says: 'When you are thinking about worrying, ask yourself whether you will still be thinking about this tomorrow, next week, or next year.'

If you decide you'll probably get over it in 24 hours, let it go. It's not that big a deal, is it? Most things fit into this category. If they don't then follow the advice on page 98 (*Fail often*).

Use this Smarty Severity Barometer whenever your pulse starts to race. Lighten up.

Not everything (in fact, very little) is that serious.
It's just your interpretation of it.

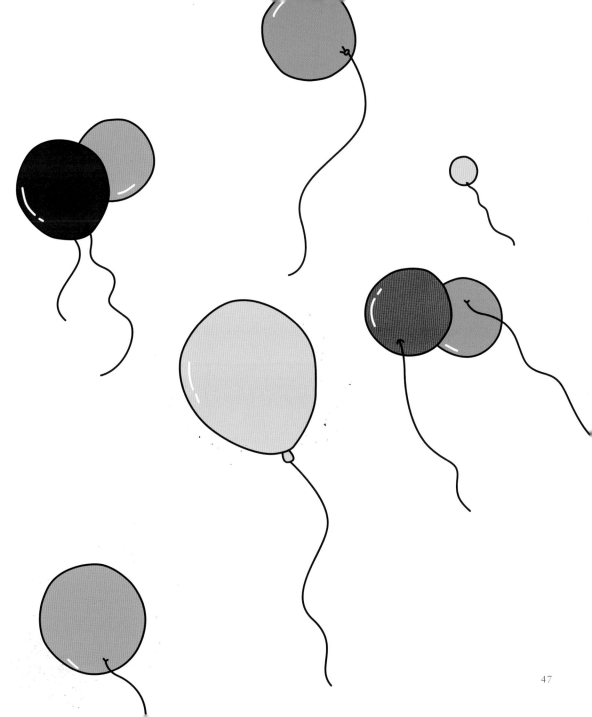

REFLECT EVERY DAY

At the end of every day ask yourself these questions that have their origins in reflective practice:

'What happened today?' Your market scan of the day
'Why did it happen?' Understand anything that needs understanding
'What one thing have I learned?' Helps you GROW
'What shall I do differently tomorrow?' Helps you commit

Giving yourself the space and time to reflect on the day's events connects the dots.

With a little distance and reflection, you'll see the bigger picture, or perceive things differently. Make joining the dots part of your daily routine.

REFLECT EVERY DAY ─────────

At the end of every day ask yourself these questions that have their origins in reflective practice:

'What happened today?' *Your market scan of the day*
'Why did it happen?' *Understand anything that needs understanding*
'What one thing have I learned?' *Helps you GROW*
'What shall I do differently tomorrow?' *Helps you commit*

Giving yourself the space and time to reflect on the day's events connects the dots.

With a little distance and reflection, you'll see the bigger picture, or perceive things differently. Make joining the dots part of your daily routine.

I'M A DUFUS

You are if you say you are.

Negative labels are a lose-lose-lose situation.

Let's say you've announced: 'I'm rubbish at social media.'

You are probably exaggerating. Chances are you're not that bad. *Lose.*

Others will see you differently. It will influence their future decisions about what to involve you in (missed learning opportunity). *Lose.*

Self-deprecation lowers the potential (or inclination) for self-growth. *Lose.*

Don't be a dufus. Don't label.* Don't be a loser.

* Yourself, or anyone else for that matter.

DEAL OF THE WEEK

You teach me & I'll teach you

VOUCHER CANNOT BE EXCHANGED FOR CASH. CHANGE GUARANTEED. DRINKS INCLUDED ON REQUEST.

DEAL OF THE WEEK

You teach me & I'll teach you

VOUCHER CANNOT BE EXCHANGED FOR CASH. CHANGE GUARANTEED. DRINKS INCLUDED ON REQUEST.

DEAL OF THE WEEK

You teach me & I'll teach you

VOUCHER CANNOT BE EXCHANGED FOR CASH. CHANGE GUARANTEED. DRINKS INCLUDED ON REQUEST.

DEAL OF THE WEEK

You teach me & I'll teach you

VOUCHER CANNOT BE EXCHANGED FOR CASH. CHANGE GUARANTEED. DRINKS INCLUDED ON REQUEST.

DEAL OF THE WEEK

You teach me & I'll teach you

VOUCHER CANNOT BE EXCHANGED FOR CASH. CHANGE GUARANTEED. DRINKS INCLUDED ON REQUEST.

DEAL OF THE WEEK

You teach me & I'll teach you

VOUCHER CANNOT BE EXCHANGED FOR CASH. CHANGE GUARANTEED. DRINKS INCLUDED ON REQUEST.

DEAL OF THE WEEK

You teach me & I'll teach you

VOUCHER CANNOT BE EXCHANGED FOR CASH. CHANGE GUARANTEED. DRINKS INCLUDED ON REQUEST.

YOUR OFFER

Sometimes you naturally assume you should be learning from others all the time. And you are.

But it is not a one-way street.

If you are a Smarty, others will learn from you, too. What do you have to offer?

Recently, I've learned from new people who have worked with me about video editing, food pop-ups and playing professional football.

People also learn when they have something to teach.

And that is pretty cool, isn't it?

KNOW WHAT MAKES YOU SEE RED

We've all got one. Probably even two, three or maybe more. Hot buttons that, when pressed, trigger a volcanic burning rage deep inside, blotting out everything else around us.

Your hot button could be a visceral dislike of selfish behaviour, or rudeness, or signs of a complete lack of empathy in the person you are speaking with. At the first hint of it, your blood will boil like hot lava and it feels quite possible steam will pour from your ears.

Calm down!

Remember they are your hot buttons, so likely to make you disproportionately see red. Recognise these hot buttons (the burning sensation is a clue). Remember what they are. It's highly likely the perceived slight is nowhere near as bad as you first thought.

Extinguish that volcano. Cool your hot buttons.

SLEEP
(but not uncontrollably)

get some EXERCISE

EAT BETTER

take a WALK

meditate

talk it over with a friend

TAILS WARN ———————

There will be hard days at work.

Your body has tons of little warning signs that tell you things are getting a bit much. Reaching for the cookie jar, unreasonable irritability, too much time at the coffee machine, forgetfulness… the list goes on.

Learn what the warning signals are for you. *Listen* and look out for them when they happen. If you're not sure, ask your friends and colleagues. They'll probably tell you!

Let the tail wag the dog on this one. Being under pressure isn't all bad, but it can be if you don't listen to the tail. And when it wags, do some of these:

BE A PRODUCTIVITY
MONSTER

MFM

My friend Lucy is a human dynamo. No sooner have we enjoyed the last coffee, or mouthful of food, on a great evening out and she'll already be organising the next big social event for our group.

Every group has a Lucy (or needs one) or nothing would ever happen. Her energy keeps things moving.

A Moving Forward Mindset (MFM) is an essential quality for a Smarty.

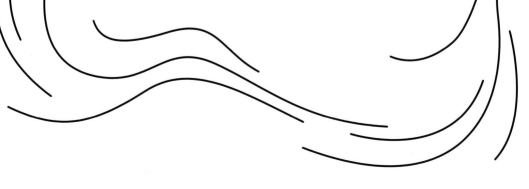

Not taking the next step to move things forward is what prevents things from happening. Smarties like things happening.

Be like Lucy. Have an **MFM**. Seize the moment: be the first to prioritise, create that action list, make that booking, have that chat or get going with whatever the Next Step is.

Moving Forward Mindset = Makes For Miracles.

BE A FARMER

There may be days where you feel you simply have 'too much' on. If you do, it's usually for only two reasons: there's a huge volume of things to do, or there's a few specific things that require dedicated, focused thinking that you haven't done yet. Both of these will rattle you.

You need a Ploughing Day.* This is a day that you behave like a farmer, get up early and get shit done. In farmer mode you will have shifted the bulk of the hard, yet routine work and/or you will be calmly thinking about major tasks to tackle.

You don't need to start work at 6am to get things done (although it is a great time of day – try it!) but an occasional Ploughing Day will reap dividends.

Tell everyone you are having a Ploughing Day. Block it out in your diary in advance. Prepare the day before, with everything lined up. List all the stuff you need to get done. Have it all ready. Zone in on the task, tune out the distractions (headphones are a great help here**) and just do it. Investing time in getting the basics out of the way leaves room for the big stuff and gets rid of the clutter preventing you from doing it.

*   I've also heard them called Quiet Days or HEDs (High Energy Days).
**I often listen to my classical music collection, which I always associate with Ploughing Days. Don't ask.

INSANITY: ——————————————→

DOING THE SAME THINGS

OVER AND OVER AGAIN

AND EXPECTING

DIFFERENT RESULTS*

* Albert Einstein did not say this, apparently!

When you don't get the result you want, the process could be wrong.
The process is often as important as the outcome, because the process gets you to it.

ENGINEER PLAY

Probably 40 per cent of what you may do in the working day is repetitive. For repetitive, read boring (but necessary). The Smarty way is to engineer.

```
/* Do this and you'll have more time to do the interesting
stuff. Imaginative thinking, upskilling on something,
or courageous leaps that propel you somewhere new.*/

/* This is not a call for ignoring the repetitive tasks on
the weekly agenda. It means engineering their completion.
They serve a purpose too. */

engineersConceive();
design() && implementSystems();

implementSystems(){
 //to make things
 workBetter() && beMoreEfficient();
}

/* TODO Take a step back. Focus on the frequently reoccurring
tasks you do. How can they run more smoothly? Could you
use technology better? Is there a call for a template or
checklist to ease the way? Is there a specific time sequence
in which to do them? */

thinkLikeAnEngineer();

pareDown() && freeYourselfUp(); // for the cool stuff.
```

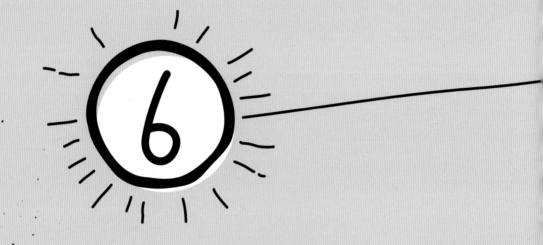

HAVE SOME SPECIAL TOOLS
IN YOUR BOX

GET THE PROBLEM STATEMENT

Forget endless meetings without hope of resolution because everyone views what's at stake differently. A Smarty looks for ways to unify. Smarties try to identify the real issue and frame it in a single statement.

A problem statement.

Problem statements clearly and succinctly set out the issue so that everyone can work towards resolving it. In one sentence it neatly summarises everything. It stops staring at the problem and articulates it. It also allows you to accurately describe what's at stake to people who were not even in the room when the issue was discussed: so no danger of anything getting lost in translation.

Reframe the conversation: make a problem statement and play it back to others for agreement.*

* For Smarties in the Advanced Class: the fewer words in a problem statement, the better in its initial phases. Try to get it down to no more than six.

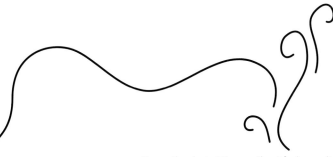

Over the last 18 months it's been like a rollercoaster.
One minute, we're moving along nicely but the next,
it's like a hurricane has hit us. Usually, it's without
any notice too, which really does impact the
quality of our work. The product is good,
and it's understandable why more
would want it. When we are better
able to plan, our team works a
whole lot better. Just last week,
Johnny was saying that...
Anna had a different take
on it though, saying...
blah ... blah ... blah
... blah ... blah ...
blah...blah...blah
... blah ...

YOUR
PROBLEM
STATEMENT
'TO ENSURE QUALITY, HOW CAN
WE MAKE SALES PREDICTABLE?'

WHAT DOES YOUR PROBLEM LOOK LIKE?

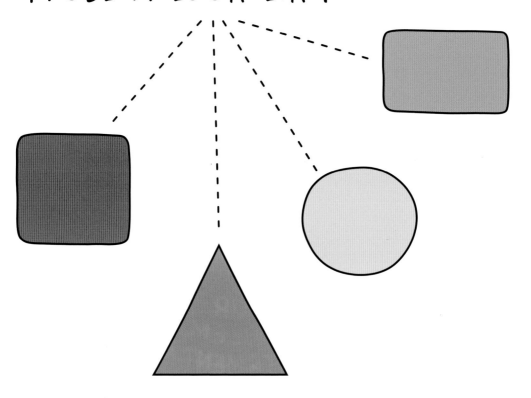

When everyone else is agonising over a challenge, Smarties make it easy.
The Smarty way is to cut short the verbal debate and convert
the conundrum into a picture.

Master just half a dozen visual techniques to deftly explain a multitude of scenarios.
You don't need to be Picasso, either. Circles indicate cycles, arrows flow, and triangles
show progression or hierarchy if you are trying to relay concepts. You can even start
to join them to make pictures if you want your scribbles to be truly memorable.

A picture is, as we all know, worth a thousand words.
Make a point without saying a word.

NO IS THE NEW Y☐S

When someone, or several people, operate above you, you won't be party to every detail of what makes your organisation tick. There are an infinite number of reasons for this: timing, confidentiality, appropriateness, irrelevance, location, anything. Just know there will always be information you don't know.

The Smarty way is to be comfortable with it. Accept you'll never always know all things. Acknowledge it, but do the best you can with the hand you've been dealt.

A counterproductive response is to make a big deal about it and say you can't move forward until you've received further information even if you've been given everything that's possible.*

There is no shame in being outside the information circle. There is, however, shame in stopping in your tracks until you're granted access. It won't always happen. Sometimes it just can't. So you'd better just get on with it.

Smarties can only control the controllables. And that's fine.

---

* It's OK to make a list of informational needs and see if they could be available. That's an *MFM mindset* (see page 60).

BETTER QUESTIONS?
BETTER ANSWERS?

Smarties are hungry for better answers. Better answers allow you to do better. How do you do better? You ask better questions. Better questions show that you care. Better questions show you are invested. Better questions help you.

You probably know the difference between open and closed questions but could you use them even better? This is where the magic happens.

Need to get to a conclusion on something? In a hurry? Need clarity? Ask CLOSED questions. They are binary. They are either/or. They are unambiguous. They are quick.

Need to scan someone's brain? Have some time on your hands? Go wide and ask OPEN questions. They encourage expansive, non-binary answers that produce a picture. They are rarely either/or. They could be ambiguous. They help you connect to someone or something in a deeper way.

Are you going to be better at asking questions now? Oops, sorry, meant to say: how are you going to be better at asking questions now?

BEAR NECESSITIES

FTSE down 20 per cent, teatime for the bears.

Whether or not you work with these terms every day, Smarties know this headline doesn't mean cut-price grub is up for the grizzlies. They also know what a 20 per cent fall in the stock market means for themselves, their company and their country. Do you?

Look up and understand the following financial terms:

- Bear and Bull markets
- Budget, Forecast
- Balance Sheet, Assets and Liabilities
- Profit and Loss (called P&L sometimes)
- Earnings before interest tax depreciation and amortization (EBITDA)
- Margin or Profit Margin
- 'The Bottom Line'
- Key Performance Indicator (KPI)

Learn what these terms mean. It's the Smarty way to mean business.

IF YOUR HEAD IS
IN THE FREEZER...

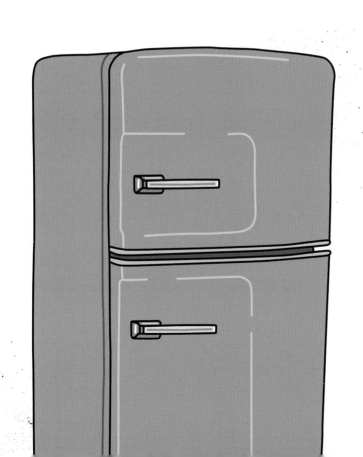

AND YOUR FEET ARE ———————————
IN BOILING WATER...

... ON AVERAGE ARE YOU OK?*

No you are not.

Question. Everything. When someone confidently quotes an impressive percentage, or makes a bold statement, make some mental checks on it. If 75 per cent adore the new product or idea, ask how many people were polled. If it was just four, then three out of the four liked the product. Is that a big enough sample to make big decisions on doubling production for the Xmas rush? Probably not.

* Comes from a popular joke amongst statisticians. I found it funny.

Likewise, lists of similar numbers and percentages quickly blur into one. Break things up once in a while: instead of '75 per cent of people want more on-the-job learning' say '3 out of 4'. It is much easier to understand and more memorable.

Never forget, either, that percentages can be a sneaky way to exaggerate facts. A company that doubles the numbers of associates every four years, increasing by 700 per cent, may only have started with one and increased to just eight. Meanwhile, a large organisation may take on 500 associates a year, but the percentage increase will remain less than 1 per cent. Doesn't sound so impressive. But it is.

Just because someone reels off statistics confidently, doesn't mean they're right or you've completely understood what the numbers really mean.

Be a Smarty statistician. Love numbers and they'll love you back.

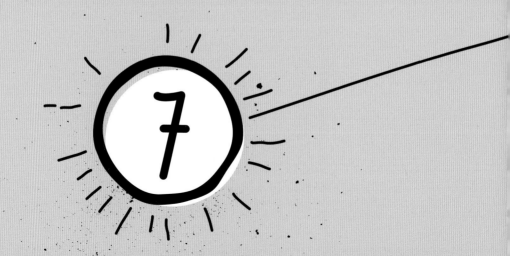

KNOW HOW YOUR BRAIN WORKS

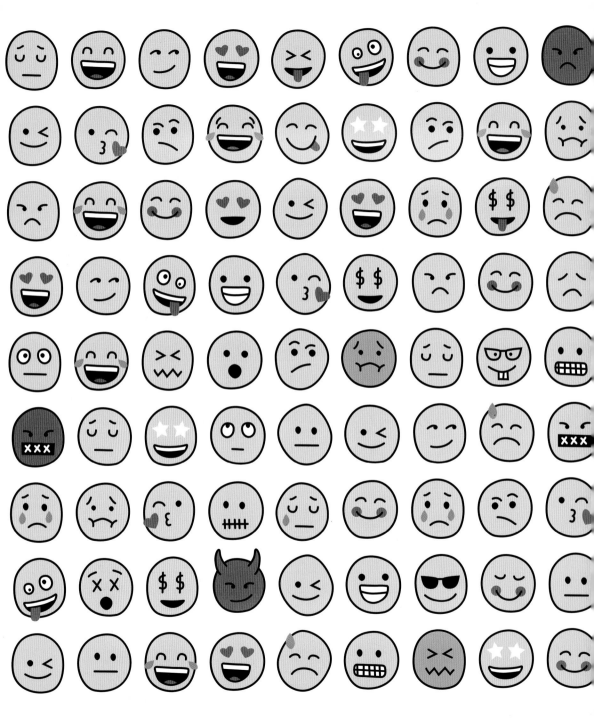

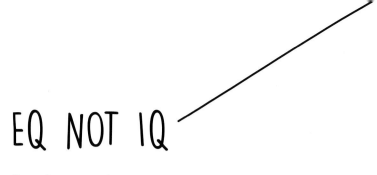

EQ NOT IQ

Smarties are not just smart.
They have a high EQ (Emotional Intelligence).

Doing well at work requires more than just intellect and IQ. Being a Smarty requires skill in handling the trickiest of beasts: emotions. That's because they can hugely impact how you behave. The thing is, emotions are not an exact science, so be ready to keep learning as you go.

Daniel Goleman, who is one of the founding fathers of EQ, has put EQ into five categories[5] and they are well worth understanding. They are:

Self-Awareness – is about you understanding your own strengths, weaknesses, emotions, needs and drivers and their impact on others. Are you self-aware?
Self-Regulation – is about maturely handling your emotions and exercising self-restraint when needed. Are you in emotional control?
Motivation – is about not solely being inspired by money or title. What drives you? How resilient and optimistic are you?
Empathy – is about compassion and an understanding of other people. Are you empathetic?
Social Skill – is about building rapport and common ground quickly. How do you manage relationships?

Know yourself. Understand others. It is the Smarty way.

AVOID TALKING ANTS

If ants could talk, do you know what they'd be saying?

'You screwed that up, didn't you?'
'You are such a loser!'
'Look at her, she managed it much better than you…'

Yeah, well, you might think. Ants DON'T talk do they?

Ah, but they do. Right into your inner ear. Around 50 to 100 times a day, according to psychologists.

By ants, I don't mean the little insects that will inevitably inherit the earth one day. Ants, according to psychologists, are Automatic Negative Thoughts. It's quite useful to visualise them as a creature, though. To give personification to that little inner voice we all have.

ANTs describe the thoughts that pop into our heads, completely unbidden, and leave behind an absolute dog's dinner of a mess of discomfort. They are masters at self-sabotage, frequently leading to a vicious circle where you become so downtrodden, or cross at your defects, you can't help but do one thing: create more.

Become a pro at recognising when you might be making thinking errors.[6]
Here are a few:

All or nothing

Only seeing black and white (and no grey).

Fortune telling

Predicting the worst possible outcome to a situation (not realising that by starting out with this attitude, you start to make it self-fulfilling).

Mind reading

Believing you know exactly what someone else is thinking.

Labelling

See I'm a dufus section (page 50).

Negative focus

Disproportionately focusing on the negative in a situation.

Disqualifying the positive

Ignoring the positive stuff in a situation.

Personalising

Investing unconnected events with personal meaning; 'My boss is in a bad mood, it must be something I have done.'

Thoughts are such tricky things. They can help you, they can hinder you, they can make you superman or they can sink you to the bottom of the ocean.

Want to ensure you are always flying high? Mastery of your thoughts starts with recognising when you are being plagued by ANTs. Argue back! Squash those ANTs! They'll never truly disappear, but you can control them.

TWO SHORT STORIES

Story one

Steve's at a conference. By a quirk of fate, he is seated next to a woman who seems pretty awesome. She introduces herself as Georgie. At the end of the day, Georgie reaches over and scribbles her number on his notes. She flashes a smile and leaves.

By the time he gets home, Steve is in turmoil.

Should he Call her?
What would he SAY?
What if she was just being "FRIENDLY"?
He asks his flatmate Mo, WHAT should he DO?
CALL HER says Mo. → Steve calls Georgie and they agree to meet.
They live happily EVER AFTER

Story two

Steve's at a conference. By a quirk of fate, he is seated next to a woman who seems pretty awesome. She introduces herself as Georgie. At the end of the day, Georgie reaches over and scribbles her number on his notes. She flashes a smile and leaves.

When Steve gets home, he goes over and over in his head whether or not to call Georgie.

His flatmate Mo wonders what's eating him.

Steve's quiet indecision goes on for days and by the time he finally makes up his mind to make the call, he's too late – Georgie's busy.

He'll never know what might have been. They don't live happily ever after.

Do yourself a favour: when you are stuck with a tough decision (or one that has emotions involved!) think what a good friend might advise you to do.[7] When we face difficult choices, our objectivity shrinks. The emotional pathways in our brains confuse our thinking. If you want a Smarty Happy Ending: get into the mindset of what a friend would advise.*

        * I nearly didn't go on my first date with my partner.
        I thought about what my sister would make me do
        because, left to my own devices, I may have bottled it.

PEAKS AND TROUGHS

Shit happens. Always.

But so do good things. All the time.

Many things in life are cyclical: economics, emotions, relationships, even the course of your day-to-day work.

Accept the peaks and troughs (sometimes they may be more pronounced, other times less so). Realise that, in the cadence of life, the trajectory of the cycle is mainly moving upwards.

Don't obsess about the downs.
Focus on moving through the ups.

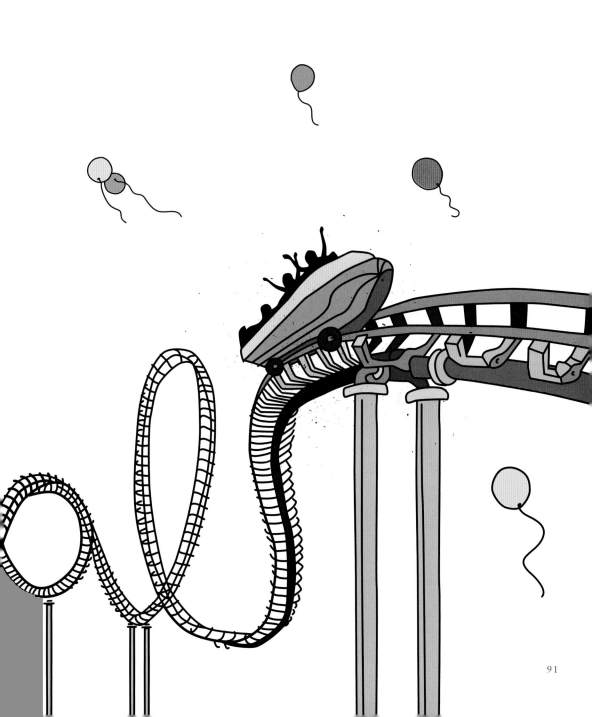

ALWAYS BE
GROWING

BE IGNORANT (ALWAYS)

The Smarty way is to fully accept you know nothing about anything.

When you know nothing, every experience is new. Guess what else happens? You listen better. This is closely linked to having a growth mindset.[8]

There is nothing wrong in saying, 'I don't know very much about this yet' or 'I'd love for you to tell me a bit more…'

People who believe they know everything about everything never change. There is zero attempt to learn and adapt. They're stuck fast in the quicksand of their own hubris.

Agile learners, aka Smarties, learn more and are generally happier.
You see, ignorance really is bliss.

x 200

Who wants to hear how great they are?
Or how well they did that piece of work?

Smarties don't.

The Smarty way is to crave feedback. Not the good stuff. The honest, gritty, this-is-how-it-could-have-been-better-and-here-is-how stuff. Feedback isn't always easy to take. But, brilliant people are brilliant at listening to feedback and asking for it.

Sometimes it won't be easy to hear. Occasionally you'll flat out disagree. Search within the feedback to find a nugget you can relate to (and there will be many). Not many people come to work wanting to hurt their colleagues. So, chances are, there is some merit in what they're saying. You just need to find it.

If you feel the need to probe (and you should), ask questions that are not defensive or accusatory. Use softer language: 'Help me to understand better'. Adjust your tone to be open and friendly. Hostility sends the signal that you're unreceptive. NEVER, EVER respond to feedback in the moment.

Thank the person who gave it to you, step back and chew on it for a while. Just as you shouldn't reject all feedback, you don't have to accept it all either. (But avoid muddying the waters by giving a string of excuses.) Weigh it up, test it against things people have said before. You'll grow as a result.

Praise feels great. But constructive feedback is praise x 200.

HAVE A DATE WITH YOURSELF——

Smarties who excel take regular time out for themselves.
Like a date – but for one.

Take yourself off for an indulgent coffee. Or a walk in the park. Anywhere where you can have a little 'me time'. Think about where you are growing to (not going to) next.

Disrupting your day-to-day environment and giving yourself time to just be will heighten your sense of self. You'll get a better feel for your skills, limitations and just how everything is going at work.

You'll be amazed at what you'll discover when you take time out to get to know yourself.

Find your off switch and be prepared to press it regularly to think about your growth.

FAIL OFTEN

Always be willing to try stuff. And to fail.

If it doesn't work, that's OK. Because you are building a formula. That formula is as important as the closely guarded one for Coca-Cola. Why? Because it's *your* formula.

Failure helps you with tons of stuff: it tells you what you're good at, what you need help with, how you deal with adversity, what to avoid, and so on. What's more, when you try something that you have previously failed at – the chances are you will do better this time around.*

Experiencing more failure is how you grow and learn. And how you learn to grow.

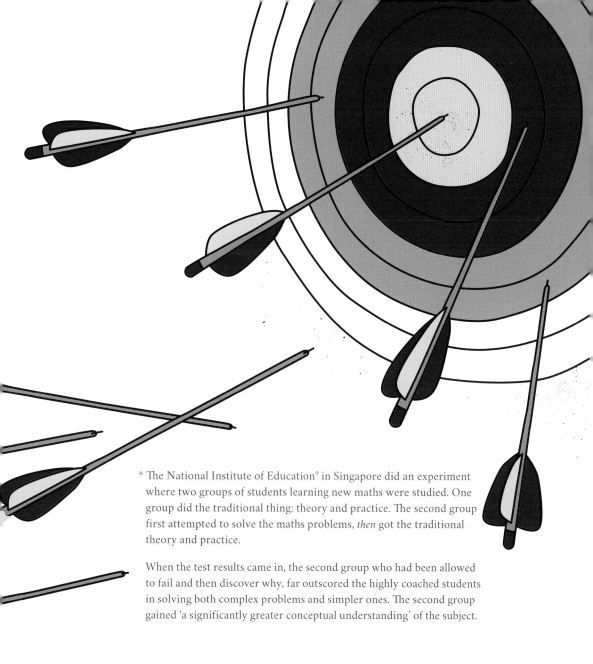

* The National Institute of Education[9] in Singapore did an experiment where two groups of students learning new maths were studied. One group did the traditional thing: theory and practice. The second group first attempted to solve the maths problems, *then* got the traditional theory and practice.

When the test results came in, the second group who had been allowed to fail and then discover why, far outscored the highly coached students in solving both complex problems and simpler ones. The second group gained 'a significantly greater conceptual understanding' of the subject.

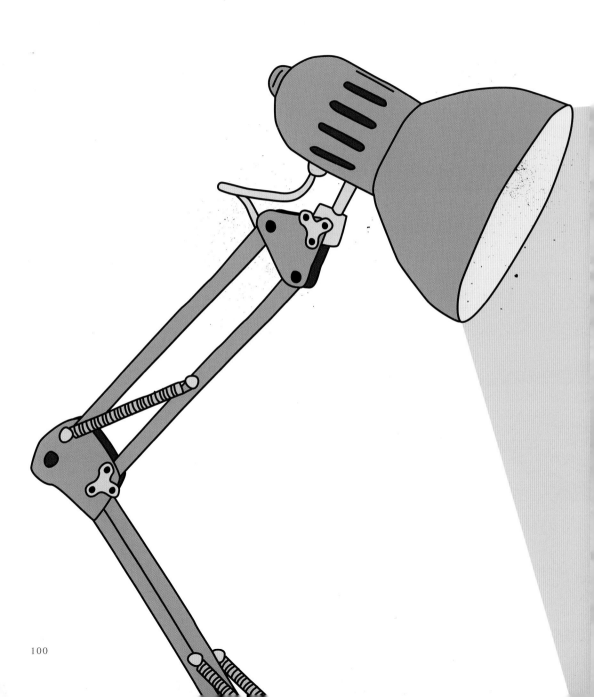

ABR (ALWAYS BE READING)

Have a need? Then read. A lot.

View reading as more than just a way to relax. It is, but it is so much more than that.

Reading is a regular for Smarties. By doing it regularly you cause a murmuring inside your own **CPU** (Central Processing Unit) that makes you more insightful, creative and empathetic.

Does this mean you should be pouring over copies of the *Economist* each night? Or working your way through the Business Management section at Amazon? You can if you like. However, a notable study has shown that *fiction* has a measurable effect on helping us understand human emotions and improving social skills too. It turns out the more Ernest Hemingway we devour, the more we expand the personality traits of extraversion, emotional stability, openness to experience, agreeableness and conscientiousness.[10]

If you don't understand any of those words, then you know what to do...
it starts with R.

GIANTS DRINK COFFEE

Smarties are Gold Card holders at Starbucks.
Do they all love coffee? Maybe.
Do they love company? Absolutely.
What type of company? The company of Wise Ones.

Being a Smarty requires you to be a master in your job and to navigate complex stuff. Doing it alone takes time and doesn't guarantee results, mostly because you're in deep and don't know what you don't know. Take the fast track and identify three Wise Ones to buy regular lattes for.

Line up at least one of the following:

Technical Wise One: These guys are the masters at their jobs. They are at the top of their technical game. They are best to talk to when you want to deepen and/or broaden your skills.

Problem-Solving Wise One: They ask great questions to help you navigate through tricky situations (or people). They help you to see solutions and options faster.

Long-Gamer Wise One: They help you escape the present, to dream and look into future. What's next for you? Where are you going? They won't spoon-feed you the answers, but they will help you to help yourself.

Wise Ones are free; but they can get quite thirsty, and even hungry, at times.

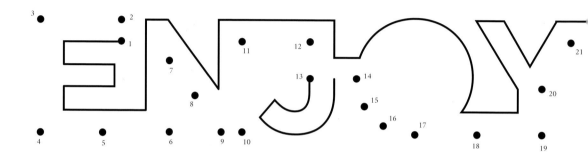

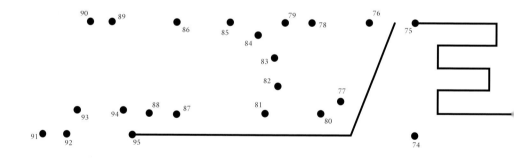

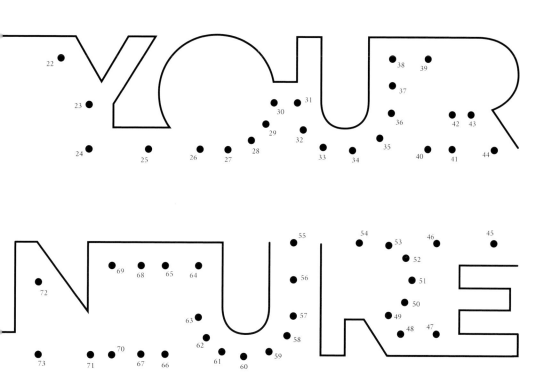

Want more?
See something. Say something. Learn something.
Or just let me know how you're doing in real life at: www.thesmartsIRL.com

THANK YOU FOR BEING WITH ME ON EVERY STEP OF THE
JOURNEY, IN WRITING, AT WORK AND EVEN IN MY DREAMS!
DON'T HAVE THE WORDS, SO MAYBE A PICTURE WILL DO.

[Khairunnisa Mohamedali; James Webber; Lucy Oates; Karen Lilje; Julia Kingsford; Andrew Baird; Riaz Shah][Alasdair Kennedy; Alastair Gill; Beth Clutterbuck; Christian Gettermann; Dan Black; David Spencer; Donna Miller; Fatim Kesvani; Graham Thompsett; Heidi Gardner; James Darley; James Penny; Jane Robinson; Joseph Gordon; Julia Harvie-Liddel; Lisa Dell'Avvocato; Maggie Stilwell; Maryam Mohamedali; Rustin Richburg; Sam Singh; Prof Sandy Pepper; Shaheen Sayeed; Steph Ahrens; Terence Perrin; Vishal Gudhka]

THANK YOU DETAILED
MANUSCRIPT READERS,
THOUGHT LEADERS AND
CHIEF ENCOURAGERS.

[Attef Gul; Charlotte Crowe; Colette Weston; David Elms; Emily Brogan; Grace Fogarty; Hawa Mansaray; Martha Morley; Sarah Cockburn; Sarah Olson; Shainy Shetty; Sita Patel; Susie Heale; Suzanne Wheatley]

THANK YOU THE
SMARTY TRAIN TEAM,
PAST AND PRESENT.

[Aaron Battista; Adam Grodecki; Alan Stirling; Alex Brackfield; Alex Skinner; Ali Tyebkhan; Alpesh Patel; Andrew Burman; Andri Stephanou; Ankeet Bajaj; Anja Stoeckigt; Anthony Lingham; Ashik Kesvani; Astad Dhunjisha; Barnaby Lenon; Barry MacEvoy; Bea Vo; Bob Athwal; Bob Gilworth; Bob Moore; Brad Christmas; Brian Hood; Brien Convery; Caroline Henderson; Catherine George; Cathy Sims; Chloe Worrall; Prof Craig Calhoun; Dan Bower; Dave Cornthwaite; Dave Ong; David Lewis;

THANK YOU TO
EVERYONE ...

... I HAVE HAD THE PLEASURE OF WORKING WITH. LEARNING FROM. ADMIRING. PROBABLY ALL THREE.

Prof Sir David Metcalf CBE; David Ramsey; David Shaw; Dominic James; Elisca Lagerweij; Emily Empel; Emma Whittaker; Eshan Kesvani; Fatema Walji; Fraser Doherty MBE; Gary Browning; George Haider; Gib Bulloch; Graham Sibley; Joel Rickett; John Glen; John Murphy; Justine Campbell; Kamal Haider; Karen Glasse; Kamran Sabir; Kashif Zafar; Kate Daubney; Laura King; Laura Yeates; Lee Warren; Leigh Clark; Lesley Campbell; Liz Wilkinson; Luke Davies; Luke Turner; Lynn Hughes; Malcolm Pemberton; Mark Bishop; Martin Butcher; Martin Corney; Michael Miller; Mustafa Khanbhai; Prof Nick Barr; Nilesh Dattani; Noor Jetha; Paul Petty; Peter Ward; Phil Sartain; Pinky Lilani CBE DL; Preet Grewal; Rafi Kesvani; Randi Zeller; Riaz Jetha; Richard Freeborn; Rob Farace; Robin Tye; Rohan Amin; Rohan Gunatillake; Ronak Mashru; Sanjay Gohil; Sarah Boddey; Sayeh Ghanbari; Sharron Green; Shawn Phillips; Shirley Jackson; Simon Bucknall; Simon Dallimore; Grey Denham; Greg Wilkinson; Griffith Jones; Gulam Kesvani; Hayley Argles-Grant; Helen Bostock; Helen Jones; Hisham Farouk; Iain Reid; Jacob Abraham; Jade Syed-Bokhari; James Alexander; James Cullens; James Taylor; Jessica Grundy; Jill Fletcher; Stewart Pope; Simon Thompson; Stanley Morrinson; Steph Morton; Steve Isherwood; Sue Hill; Susan Keane; Sujatha Zafar; Suzy Syle; Tom Kalaris; Tom Mercer; Prof Tim Broyd; Tim Cattell; Victoria Hyland; Vicram Sharma; Vivek Sarohia; Prof Wendy Carlin; Will Gompertz; Zain Mohamedali; Zoha Jetha]

Notes

1. Google online article: 'Planning, Productivity and Progress – The Power of P', Cleve Gibbon

2. Galinsky, A. D., Magee, J. C., Inesi, M. E., & Gruenfeld, D. H. (2006). 'Power and perspectives not taken'. *Psychological Science*, 17(12)

3. Danziger, S., Levav, J., & Avnaim-Pesso, L. (2011). 'Extraneous factors in judicial decisions'. *Proceedings of the National Academy of Sciences*, 108(17)

4. Kross, E., Bruehlman-Senecal, E., Park, J., Burson, A., Dougherty, A., Shablack, H., ... & Ayduk, O. (2014). 'Self-talk as a regulatory mechanism: How you do it matters'. *Journal of Personality and Social Psychology*, 106(2)

5. Goleman, D. (2004). 'What makes a leader?' *Harvard Business Review*, 82(1)

6. These come from the work of Aaron Beck and his former student David Burns. Chapter 3 of Burns's book, *Feeling Good: The New Mood Therapy* (1980), William Morrow and Company, goes into some great detail

7. For more on how your mind works on making decisions, see Chip and Dan Heath's book *Decisive* (2013), Currency. Thanks Dan and Chip – I might not have met my partner without it!

8. For more on this, read up on Carol Dweck's excellent work on growth and fixed mindsets: *Mindset* (2006), Random House. You'll want to have a Growth Mindset

9. Read more about Productive Failure (PF) and the experiment on Professor Manu Kapur's website, www.manukapur.com

10. Maja Djikic, Keith Oatley, Sara Zoeterman & Jordan B. Peterson, (2009), 'On being moved by art: How reading fiction transforms the self'. *Creativity Research Journal*, 21(1)